The First Seeing Eye Dogs

By Burnham Holmes

Illustrated by Judith Clark

cpi
contemporary perspectives, inc.

This book is distributed by Silver Burdett Company, Morristown, New Jersey, 07960.

Library of Congress Number: 78-14804

Art and Photo Credits

Cover illustration by Judith Clark
Photos on pages 23, 46, 47, and 48 courtesy of The Seeing Eye, Inc.
Photo on page 33, ACME (UPI)
Every effort has been made to trace the ownership of all copyrighted material in this book and to obtain permission for its use.

Library of Congress Cataloging in Publication Data

Holmes, Burnham, 1942-
The first seeing eye dogs.

SUMMARY: Discusses some of the early efforts in training dogs to guide the blind in Switzerland and later in the United States, focusing on the relationship of Morris Frank and his dog Buddy who pioneered needed changes for traveling blind people in this country.
1. Guide dogs — Juvenile literature. [1. Guide dogs. 2. Frank, Morris, 1907 *or* 8 — 3. Blind] I. Title.
HV1780.S4H65 362.4'1 78-14804
ISBN 0-89547-045-4

Manufactured in the United States of America
ISBN 0-89547-045-4

Contents

Chapter I

A New Way for the Blind to "See"

It was Germany. The year was 1916 and World War I was raging. A young German corporal was cut off from his unit behind French lines. He was trying to find his way back. Suddenly, a shell blew up near him. He hit the ground — but not quickly enough. A piece of the shell hit him in the face. When he opened his eyes, he could see nothing. The young soldier was blinded.

Frightened and screaming in pain, the blind soldier moved about on his hands and knees for hours. He crawled in the direction he thought his army unit might be. Hours later, tired and weak from loss of blood, he crawled into a nearby shell hole. There, he passed out.

A German army doctor was making his rounds on the front lines. He was working on his last wounded soldier. Suddenly, his German shepherd dog, Excelsior, began to whine gently and sniff at the air.

"What's the matter, boy? What do you smell? Go find out!"

Let off his leash, Excelsior ran off some 200 yards. He went beyond the field hospital and stopped at a hole made by a shell. The doctor watched his dog through field glasses. He could see him pulling at something. Finally, he saw a young German soldier struggle to his feet. Excelsior was helping him by tugging at his sleeve.

The army doctor could see that the soldier was having trouble walking. The man was badly hurt. Excelsior was now leading him between deep holes and around barbed wire. Suddenly, the doctor knew what he was watching. This soldier could not see — he seemed completely blind. And a *dog* was leading him to safety. The soldier walked a few steps, then stopped. He would not move again until Excelsior pulled him forward a few more feet.

"Good dog, Excelsior! Hang on, soldier, I'm a doctor. I'm coming to help you!"

The young corporal had finally made it back safely. But he knew he owed his very life to an alert and helpful German shepherd dog!

Months later, the army doctor was still thinking about his dog's amazing rescue. "If a dog like Excelsior can do this, imagine what a trained dog could do for the blind!" And with this thought in mind, this doctor, whose name we do not know, started a new school in Potsdam, Germany. It was a school for dogs — dogs who would learn how to see for people who could not see for themselves. It was the first school of its kind, but it was not the last.

How on earth can that dog keep from getting hit? This is the worst street in Potsdam. And that dog is leading a blind woman through the traffic!

These were the thoughts of Dorothy Eustis. She was an American who lived in Switzerland. Dorothy and her husband trained German shepherds for police and Red Cross work. Now she was visiting a German school for guide dogs. Her husband George had visited the school. He could not believe the amazing work of its dogs. He wrote to his wife and begged her to come to Germany right away.

Mrs. Eustis certainly knew that German shepherds were smart dogs. She had seen the wonderful work of

Red Cross dogs during the war. She had trained shepherds to guard buildings and protect people and property for the police. But she could never have believed what she was seeing here in Potsdam. Dogs were leading their blind owners across busy streets in perfect safety. Dogs were guiding people on long trips to places they had never been before.

Watching that guide dog leading the way for a blind man made a believer out of Dorothy Eustis. It was a sight she would never forget. When Dorothy and George got back to Fortunate Fields, their Swiss school for dogs, they felt they had to tell others about what they had seen. "Maybe we can bring such a school to America," Dorothy said. And she sat down to write a news story about the German dogs who helped the blind to find their way. She called it "The Seeing Eye." On November 5, 1927, millions of Americans read the story in a well known magazine of that time, the *Saturday Evening Post*.

Chapter 2

I Want One of Those Dogs!

"Listen to the article in this magazine!" said Mr. Frank. "It's called 'The Seeing Eye,' by Dorothy Eustis." Mr. Frank, a middle-aged man, was sitting in the living room of his home in Nashville, Tennessee. It was 1927 and he was talking with his son, Morris. He often read to the boy, but this news story was one he knew Morris would find most interesting.

To everyone, I think, there is always something particularly pathetic about a blind man. In darkness and uncertainty he must start again, wholly dependent on outside help for every move. His other senses may rally to his aid, but they cannot replace his eyesight. To man's never failing friend has been accorded this special privilege. Ladies and gentlemen, I give you the German shepherd!

Morris Frank sat quietly as his father read the rest of the story. Morris was 19 years old. He had been blind for the last three years. He lost one eye in a horseback-riding accident when he was only six years old. Ten years later, when he was 16, he lost his other eye. That happened in a boxing match. Life without sight was not easy, but Morris tried hard not to feel sorry for himself. He just wanted to be able to do more things for himself — to get around without being helped by others.

All that night Morris Frank thought about the news story his father had read. He talked with his mother for hours about what a guide dog might do for him. He remembered how much help he had needed from others over the last years. First he needed someone to help him to get to classes in school. Then he needed people to help him around his hometown of Nashville. Now he needed help every day to do his work. Morris sold life insurance.

Morris was too excited to sleep much that night. He decided not to waste another minute dreaming of what might happen. He would take steps to make sure

THE SATURDAY
EVENING POST

something *did* happen. Morris sat down and typed a letter to Dorothy Eustis:

> *Is what you say true? If so, I want one of those dogs! Thousands of blind people like me hate being dependent on others. Help me and I will help them. Train me and I will bring back my dog and show people how a blind man can be on his own. How can I help to bring these dogs to blind Americans? How can I help to give all those who want it a chance at a new life?*

But after mailing the letter the next morning Morris began to have second thoughts. After all, Switzerland was a long way from Nashville. Was it worth the money and time to go there? Perhaps it would be easier to simply accept his blindness as a fact of life — to go on the way he was. That was when his mother quickly stepped in.

Mrs. Frank told Morris he had to make the trip if he had the chance. "You have a long life ahead of you," she said. "Take a chance. Not only for yourself, but for others who are blind." Morris knew how much this meant to his mother. Mrs. Frank, too, was completely blind.

A few weeks later Morris had an answer to his letter. Mrs. Eustis said she and her husband worked with a good trainer by the name of Jack Humphrey. They had great dogs and a good school. They had been much moved by Morris's words. On her next trip to the United States Dorothy Eustis called Morris Frank. If he would travel all the way to Switzerland, she would help him. Her husband George, Jack Humphrey, and a dog named Kiss would be waiting for him. Did he still want to come?

Did he? In the spring of 1928, Morris was on the *Ansonia*, a British ship bound for Europe. His heart jumped wildly as he felt the great ship move from the dock. He thought he heard his mother and father shouting over the noisy crowd.

Then, standing alone in the salty wind, Morris Frank felt only one thought enter his world of darkness. "Soon, I will not stand alone. Soon — very soon — I will have the eyes of a new friend to help me see!"

Chapter 3

Morris Makes a Friend for Life

The trip over was not a happy one for Morris. Twice a day he was led around the deck of the ship. At night he was locked in his cabin so as not to hurt himself.

As if this wasn't bad enough, the worst part of the trip came when he reached France. Morris was led from the ship. He was left alone on the dock and told to wait right there. But more than an hour passed and no one came for him. All alone and afraid to move a step, Morris felt helpless. He called out but no one came. Finally someone walked by and asked where he was going. "Paris," Morris said. "Please help me. I am blind." He was just able to hold back the tears in his eyes.

In Paris Morris was led to his hotel room. Once again, he was locked in to keep him safe. But when he was hungry no one came with food. He felt around the room for a telephone. But he could not find anyone who spoke English at the other end. He fell asleep until morning when he awoke to a knock on the door. A friend of Dorothy Eustis's had come to take him to the train.

By the time he got off the train and met Dorothy Eustis in Switzerland, Morris had made up his mind. He knew what he wanted. A guide dog! Never again would he be afraid to be alone. Never again would he need others to help him take care of himself.

The next day at lunch Morris met everyone who lived at Fortunate Fields. George Eustis and Jack Humphrey watched Morris closely as he ate. They saw the trouble he had spreading butter on bread and cutting his meat. They saw him search for his food with his fingers. They could feel his anger over not being able to eat his food easily. They now knew the dog they would choose for Morris. Two German shepherds had been trained — Gala and Kiss. Both dogs were smart and right for the job. But for someone as frightened as this young man, a very gentle dog would be needed. They chose Kiss.

Jack Humphrey talked with Morris after lunch. He told him some of the problems they had in training a

guide dog for the blind. And he told Morris some of the problems he would have in using the dog. "We use only female dogs for the blind," he said. "The males are used in police and army work."

"We have to make sure that a guide dog will not be frightened by crowds or noise," Jack Humphrey went on. "She can't go running off after other dogs or animals. She has to think only of you. She has to know when there is danger ahead, and she has to keep you away from it."

Morris listened as Jack told him the way Kiss had been trained to stop at curbs and stop to wait for traffic lights. He could not believe that a dog could do his thinking for him. But he really became worried when Jack said, "Just remember, Morris, she isn't your dog. You belong to her! If she doesn't like you, she won't want to guide you."

Morris spent the rest of the day with Kiss. "You will get to like me, old girl. You'll see. But first, let's change your name to something that won't sound as silly as Kiss. From now on, your name is Buddy." Calling her by her new name, Morris gave Buddy some meat, as Jack had said to do. And that very night Buddy crawled up on Morris's bed, keeping a lonely blind man warm in the cold room. Morris smiled as he fell asleep with his hand on Buddy's head.

Chapter 4

A Guide Dog Learns Her Job

Jack Humphrey and George Eustis began training Buddy months before Morris ever got to Fortunate Fields. They followed a training program much like the one they had seen at Potsdam. It was really three programs, and they started when Buddy was about 14 months old.

First they trained the dog as many people try to train any puppy. Over and over they told the bright German shepherd what to do. Each time they showed her exactly what they wanted. If she did what they wanted, they would pet her and speak kindly to the dog. When she did not do what was asked, she would hear the trainer call "No" or "Pfui" (a Swiss word that means "no good"). To a well-trained dog it is always more fun to please the trainer — to get more pats and fewer "pfuis."

Soft dogs are the ones who give up after hearing "pfui" too many times. Buddy proved to be a "hard" dog — she never stopped trying to please, learning how to get more praise from her trainer. Buddy was soon ready for part two of the program.

A good guide dog must quickly obey everything it hears from its blind master. Most dogs that pass the first part of their training easily pass this part. Buddy was taught certain words that must be instantly understood. "Buddy — *come!*" meant that the dog had to quickly move to the trainer's side. "Lie down" ... "sit up" ... "stand" ... and "find it for me" were orders that had to be quickly obeyed.

Now came the final program — the one that turns a well-trained dog into a guide dog for the blind. A special U-shaped harness was placed over Buddy's body. The harness fit so that Buddy could move easily. The dog would now have to get used to someone holding the U-shaped handle at all times. The person holding that handle would be blind and would someday go wherever Buddy would lead.

A well-trained dog gets some kind words from her trainer.

For this part of the training Jack Humphrey acted as if he were blind. If Buddy led him under a low bridge, Jack would hit his head. If Buddy led him too close to other people or walls or trees, Jack would be bumped. Day by day Buddy learned how much room to leave above Jack and on his sides. Soon her "blind" trainer was moving from place to place without bumping his head or walking into things.

But the most important part of the program was yet to come. No matter how good Buddy was, she would never be the right guide dog for Morris Frank if she could not learn to stop at every curb on the street. A guide dog for the blind must bring the blind person to the street corner and wait for the next order — "turn left" . . . "turn right" . . . or "forward." Only dogs as smart as Buddy can pass this part of the program. The seeing eye dog must be able to think a situation through and guide her blind master.

Jack would fall at a curb when Buddy did not stop early enough. "PFUI, Buddy" would be enough to make Buddy remember at the next curb. Now that Buddy was stopping on time, Jack would say "forward," even when something was in the way. It was up to Buddy to stay put — not to move until the car or truck had gone by and the way was clear. When Buddy was doing her best thinking — watching for dangers, finding doors, and understanding which

places were too low, too narrow, or too high — Jack knew she was ready to work with her blind master.

A tongue licked Morris's face. Today Buddy was ready to start their training together.

"Always keep the dog on your left side," Jack told Morris. "She should be between you and the traffic." Morris called "forward." Buddy started off, almost dragging Morris to the cable car for the ride into town. "Make sure Buddy's feet are out of the way of the other passengers," warned Jack. "Just as you are protected by her, you must do everything to make life better for her."

Jack told Morris what to do at every turn. Buddy knew what to do, but Morris didn't. "Tell Buddy what to do in a clear, firm voice," Jack reminded him. "And tell her, 'That's a good girl,' when she does something right. She wants this to work as much as you do."

For the next week, Buddy and Morris always worked with Jack close by. Then they were on their own as Jack followed at a distance. One day when Buddy and Morris were in town, they ran into trouble. Morris suddenly heard Jack shout: "Runaway horses!" Morris froze, not knowing what to do. But Buddy did

not stand still. She quickly pulled Morris up a steep hill at the side of the road. The horses and wagon raced over the spot where Morris had been standing just a few seconds before.

"That's a *good girl!*" Morris cried when he heard the horses clatter by. Buddy licked his face and wagged her tail in agreement.

Buddy had begun to understand that this was no longer just a game. Her new master was different from the trainer. Buddy seemed to know that Morris was blind and needed her to make many decisions.

Once, after a month of training had passed, Morris asked to go to a barbershop. "Go yourself!" snapped Jack. "What's your dog for?" Jack then explained the route — counting the blocks and turns for Morris.

For a lot of people haircuts are easy to get. But not so for Morris. It was quite a job that day, his first trip alone with Buddy. Morris thoroughly enjoyed the trip, including every right and left turn. That night at dinner he started laughing and couldn't stop.

"What's so funny?" asked Mrs. Eustis. She looked over at Jack who shrugged his shoulders.

"Nothing. Absolutely nothing," replied Morris. "It's a little thing, I guess, getting a haircut. But today is

27068

the happiest day I can remember. Somehow I feel less blind and more like everybody else with normal sight. I feel free."

"You know, you're going to be leaving us soon," said Dorothy Eustis sadly. "I've been thinking about what you said in your letter. There are two things that you must do before we can begin helping other blind people in the United States. First, you must show that a blind person and a guide dog can get around the busy city streets over there. And second, guide dogs must be able to walk into all public places. Otherwise, how can a blind person ever lead a normal life?"

"If you can see to these two things, I'll start a school in America for training guide dogs. It's up to you." Dorothy paused and smiled. "And, of course, Buddy."

Underneath the table, Morris felt Buddy wag her tail and place her head on his knee.

Chapter 5

Buddy Becomes Famous

On the boat trip back to the United States Buddy and Morris were familiar figures on deck, even at the captain's table. They probably made more friends in the first few minutes than Morris had made on his entire trip earlier that year.

When the ship docked in America, the many reporters present on the pier challenged Buddy and Morris to cross the street known as "death street." It was West Street, a crowded street filled with fast-moving cars and trucks. If Morris could have seen all the traffic, he might have said no. But he needed to show how well a guide dog could lead a blind man around the city streets. What better way was there than to cross the busiest street in New York City in full view of newspaper reporters?

Buddy looked back as if to ask, "Do you really want to do this?" But there was something about Morris and the reporters standing nearby that told Buddy that this was very important. So, she moved out into the sea of heavy trucks and buses. She led Morris around the taxicabs darting in and out along the curb. After a struggle that was much like swimming through strong ocean waves, Buddy and Morris crossed to the other side of the street. The reporters broke into cheers. Many of them had long ago given up trying to get across the dangerous street themselves.

Buddy and Morris traveled to many cities on their way home to Nashville. And everywhere they went reporters would follow.

Usually Buddy and Morris traveled the country by train. After showing Morris to his seat, the conductors would lead Buddy away to the baggage car. Morris did not like the idea of not being able to keep Buddy with him. But rules were rules and he went along with them. Then, one night, a conductor urged Morris to come with him. "Fast! Your dog is loose!" When Morris entered the baggage car, the door accidently locked behind him. After calling the conductor for several minutes, he knew that it was no use. The conductor was gone. Buddy and Morris were both locked in for the night. "Why sir," said the conductor the next morning, "you've been sleeping on a coffin!"

The railroad rule against guide dogs was also the rule in other public places. Once at a restaurant the headwaiter came around to thank Morris for leaving

Buddy leads Morris Frank across a crowded street in 1933. ▶

TEL.

Buddy in the coatroom. Morris then lifted up the tablecloth. There, under the table, was Buddy.

Finally, after a journey of many weeks and many thousands of miles, Buddy and Morris arrived in Nashville. The first thing Morris did was to stop off at the telegraph office. His one-word telegram to Dorothy Eustis said it all: "SUCCESS."

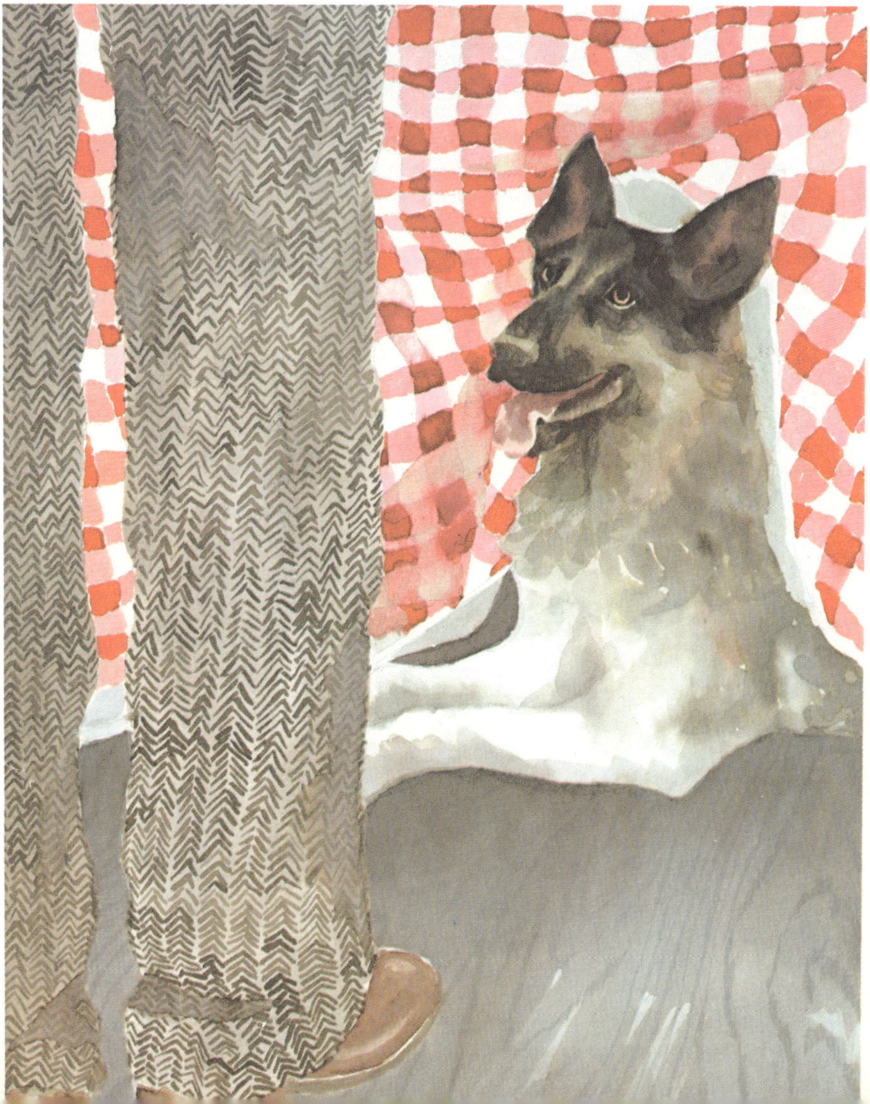

Chapter 6

The Seeing Eye Comes to America

True to her word, in 1929 Dorothy Eustis visited the United States again. It was a very special visit this time. Mrs. Eustis, her husband, and Jack Humphrey had spent a lot of time planning a school for blind people and guide dogs. It would be called The Seeing Eye, and it would be in Morris Frank's hometown of Nashville, Tennessee. There was much work to be done.

Jack Humphrey would have quite a time finding the right dogs. Teachers would be even harder to find. The school would start with German shepherds and trainers from Fortunate Fields in Switzerland. That would give Jack time to find some more of both in America. But dogs and teachers were not the only problem. The Seeing Eye would also need some money.

Mrs. Eustis went to well-to-do friends, strangers, clubs — anyone who might offer money for the school. When people asked if the idea could really work, meeting Morris and Buddy was enough of an answer for most. That was the case with the president of an insurance company. "How can a dog know a red light from a green one?" was one question he asked. He would give the school money, but he wanted some answers first.

"A dog tells the red signal from the green just the way a color-blind person would," Morris answered. "The red light is always on top. But the seeing eye dog does even better crossing streets than most people. She watches the cars around her as well as the traffic light. So even if Buddy had the green light with her, she would not step in front of a car running a red light."

When it was time to go Morris found that Buddy had been sitting in the insurance man's chair instead of lying on the floor. "That's a bad girl!" he said.

"She's no bad girl," said the insurance man. "All the time you were talking she was looking at me. I'm

giving you a large check for The Seeing Eye. And I'm giving you the money because of what Buddy was telling me with her eyes."

While Dorothy Eustis, Morris, and Buddy were busy raising money, Jack Humphrey kept after the problem of finding dogs and trainers. He begged an old friend, Willi Ebeling, to come to Nashville from his home in New Jersey. When Ebeling said he would come, Jack Humphrey knew he had found the dogs he would need. Mr. Ebeling had trained German shepherds for years, and now he could turn them into seeing eye dogs.

A new problem had come up for the people of The Seeing Eye. The blind students and the trainers loved Nashville, but their hard work was even harder in the heat of the long southern summer there. Mr. Ebeling, however, came up with an answer. The Seeing Eye would move to his home in Morristown, New Jersey. His dogs could be trained at home. The blind students could live at a nearby hotel in town.

If there were still people who wondered if dogs could really help the blind, the move to Morristown told the whole story. Soon after the move there was a fire in the hotel where the blind students lived. Every one of them was led safely from the hotel by a seeing eye dog. All the blind students and dogs were waiting outside the hotel when the firemen arrived!

Chapter 7

A Light in the Darkness

The Seeing Eye and Buddy were becoming famous everywhere. Presidents Calvin Coolidge and Herbert Hoover invited Buddy to visit the White House. Stories about Buddy were broadcast on radio shows. People crowded into theaters where Buddy performed on the stage. And soon many blind people wanted dogs and the training to use them.

By 1935, every U.S. railroad had opened its doors to seeing eye dogs. The blind could now travel farther from home — *on their own.* City after city was passing laws allowing seeing eye dogs in restaurants, parks, buses, trains — all public places. At last, there was some light in the dark world of the blind!

Buddy's tenth birthday was in 1936. She was very sick that year and it took a long time for Morris Frank and his parents to nurse her back to health. Later that same year, Buddy paid the Frank family back for their help. She saved Morris's life!

One day, after making a speech to raise money for The Seeing Eye, Morris went swimming in a nearby lake. He knew there was a raft straight out from where he had stepped into the water. Buddy sat on the shore and watched Morris swim for the raft. Suddenly, Buddy saw Morris was in trouble. He couldn't find the raft. Tired and frightened, Morris was drowning!

Buddy jumped into the water. The old seeing eye dog was still weak after being ill for so long. But she swam long and hard to reach her blind master. She led Morris back to shore where he fell over — weak, but still alive. In the months that followed, however, it was clear that the effort had been too much for Buddy. She was sick most of the next year.

By 1938, Morris Frank went after the new and growing airlines. Seeing eye dogs were not allowed on airplanes. Morris would change all that, and Buddy would help him.

Morris asked many newspaper friends to ask the airlines to let seeing eye dogs on airplanes. He had

already found someone at United Airlines to let him buy a ticket for Buddy. Now he wanted reporters and photographers to be there when he and Buddy walked up the steps to the airplane.

The big moment came. But Buddy was so sick that Morris had to carry her up the airplane steps. Many of the news people watched with tears in their eyes. A short time later, Buddy died. But she was alive long enough to prove that blind people could get around in airports and airplanes. All they needed was a seeing eye dog to help them.

LINES

Chapter 8

Seeing Eye Dogs Today

Since its beginnings in Nashville, The Seeing Eye has trained many thousands of guide dogs. And many more kinds than German shepherds are trained to lead the blind. In all, 29 different breeds of dogs have been used. But the German shepherd is still the most popular, followed by Labrador and golden retrievers.

In order to train with a guide dog a blind person must be in good health, be between the ages of 16 and 50 years old, and have a need for a guide dog.

While it costs The Seeing Eye from $3,000 to $4,000 to train a guide dog, a blind person never has to pay more than $150 for a dog. The Seeing Eye pays the rest out of money given by people who want the school's good work to continue.

Today there are many groups that train guide dogs and the blind people they will lead. The Seeing Eye is, of course, the oldest. It is also the largest. But every such group owes an everlasting debt of thanks to Morris Frank, Dorothy and George Eustis, Jack Humphrey, Willi Ebeling, and one more ... Buddy, the first seeing eye dog!

Today blind people take part in many sports and go almost anywhere with their guide dogs.